The Advanced Options Trading Guide

I0477704

The Best Complete Guide for Earning Income with Options Trading, Learn Secret Investment Strategies for Investing in Stocks, Futures, ETF, Options, and Binaries.

By Neil Sharp

Table of Contents

Introduction

Thank you for purchasing *The Advanced Options Trading Guide. The Best Complete Guide for Earning Income with Options Trading, Learn Secret Investment Strategies for Investing in Stocks, Futures, ETF, Options, and Binaries*. I am sure that this book will live up to your expectations.

If you have purchased this book, it is because you are interested in learning more about options trading and how this type of trading can help you make a profit as a result of your investment activities.

As you will see in the following pages, this book contains a wealth of information that you will not find readily available anywhere else. In fact, many of the concepts found in this book are not easily found in a single volume. Often, you would have to consult numerous sources in order to find all of this information in a single source.

You will also find that options trading is an extensive topic. But fear not, we will go step by step in such a way that grasping these concepts will not be as hard as you think. If you happen to have prior knowledge with some understanding of this topic, then I am sure that you will find a clear understanding of the options trading markets. If you are already familiar with this topic, then I hope that you will find new information that will help you expand your current knowledge and gain a fresh perspective on this matter.

Options trading differs somewhat from regular equities trading. With equities, you were dealing with publicly traded companies. Of course, the options market also deals with publicly traded companies but the difference lies in that options are considered part of the derivatives market. As such, the derivatives market is far larger and far more complicated than the traditional equities market.

Consequently, it will certainly help you to learn more about how the derivatives market works, especially since there are many opportunities available for investors in derivatives. So don't be intimidated by the vast amount of information available out there with reference to the derivatives market. In reading this book, I hope that you get a clear idea of how the derivatives market, through options trading, can open up newer opportunities for investors such as yourself.

For most professional investors, options are a common tool that is used to help protect themselves from volatile markets and sudden swings in the prices of equities and commodities. This is why it is important to also understand the nature of equities and commodities.

Since options are considered derivatives, you are not exactly trading an equity or commodity, that is, a specific security that is attached to the contract which you are negotiating. That's being said, it is vital to have a clear perspective on the dynamics of each market.

Each of the chapters in this book is dedicated to illustrating how each of these markets interacts in such a way that a broader structure is revealed as part of the global structure of financial markets.

The good thing about all of this is that highly technical knowledge is not required. All you need is some time and dedication in order for you to gain a considerable grasp of the concepts discussed throughout this book.

So buckle up because we are going to drill down into the concepts which make up the options trading markets and thereby broader financial markets, not just in the United States, but also around the world. Bear in mind the teas are global markets we are talking about. So keeping an open mind and the global perspective are fundamental tools in understanding how the dynamics of the options trading market works.

Chapter 1: What are Options?

In this chapter, we are going to drill down on the basics of options and how these types of investments work in the overall scheme of financial markets. It must be pointed out that options are not investment vehicles in themselves.

What does that mean?

For example, when you purchase a stock, you're purchasing a piece of a company. That is, you are purchasing partial ownership of a publicly traded company. And while stock is not a tangible asset which you can hold in your hands, it is proof that you own a hard asset, in this case, a company.

So, when dealing with options, you are dealing with a number of transactions which have an underlying asset supporting them. However, this type of investment fits the description and definition of a derivative. This is why the options trading market tends to be a bit more complex than the traditional equities market.

But before we dig any deeper into options themselves, let's get some important definitions out of the way.

First of all, this book does not deal in securities trading. As such, we are not talking about stocks and bonds. When you talk about securities in general, you are talking about ownership of real assets which you can then convert into cash in the regular markets.

For instance, if you purchase stock in a company, you can then turn around and sell that stock to another investor. Whether you make or lose money is dependent on market forces. Consequently, you must be clear on what price you are purchasing a security and at what price you are going to be selling it. Nevertheless, stocks are highly liquid assets because you can trade them virtually anytime you want, and you will always find a buyer for them.

Unless you have purchased stock into a company that has completely tanked, you will always find investors who are willing to take on stock even in a down market. This is what I mean when I say that stocks are highly liquid assets.

Another type of highly liquid assets contained under the securities umbrella is bonds. Bonds are also highly liquid assets that can be sold immediately when you need cash. Of course, if you have purchased bonds of a nation which is in default, then such bonds will essentially be worthless. So long as you invest in high-quality bonds, you will always have an asset which you can convert into cash at any moment.

With this definition, I hope to illustrate what a security is. Please feel free to check out any of the other books in this series which deal on the topic of equities markets and stock trading. I am sure these books will provide you with a wealth of information that you can put to use right away as you find your bearings as an investor.

One other thing before we move on to defining what an option is, trading in options is a speculative activity that yields good results but does not come without significant risk. That is why I would encourage you to do your homework at all times so that you are sure that the investments you are making will provide you with the opportunity to protect yourself against such risks.

Defining "Options"

An option, simply put, is a financial contract that locks in the right to buy or sell but not an obligation.

What this implies, is that an option is exactly as what its name suggests: it is a choice, not an obligation. As such, you as an investor can choose to lock in a given price for the contract, but you are not obligated to carry out with the transaction.

As a result, you have the option of backing out of the contract if, for some reason, you choose to do so. For instance, it could be that you have a cash flow problem and you run out of money. So, you can't go through with the contract unless you find the money to make the deal happen.

Granted, most transactions in the derivatives market don't necessarily involve cash, but you do need to have some type of liquidity in order to make the deal go through. In other cases, circumstances change, and you may no longer become interested in that particular asset which you took the option out on.

Now, the reason why we say that options are derivatives is because you are not actually trading the asset itself, but rather, you are entering a contract which is based on an underlying asset. Since an option is a contract in which you have the right to buy or sell—that is one contract, the actual purchase or sale is a separate contract.

I hope you can see that when an option goes through, it is actually two, separate contracts that kick in. The reason for this is because you could actually make the deal without enacting the options contract.

Allow me to illustrate.

Let's assume that your company does a lot of business overseas. It is based in the US and the majority of its business is in Europe. So, your company is naturally worried about exchanged rates between the US Dollar and the Euro. Since there is a high degree of uncertainty surrounding the Euro at the moment due to the Brexit, you are concern about exchange rates affecting your business deals.

In two months, you will collect a sizeable sum of money which will come due as per the expiration of a contract. Your business partner will make the payment in Euros as per the agreement. But your company is concerned that if the Euro falls because of the Brexit, then you will actually be left with less money once you convert it back to US Dollars.

In other words, if the Euro tanks, you will receive less US dollars when you convert that payment from Euros back into US Dollars.

Therefore, this concern has led your company's directors to consider taking out an options contract with a local financial institution that will underwrite the contract locking in a fixed exchange rate. What this does is protect your company's income in case the Euro should tank.

Consequently, there are two possible outcomes: one, the Euro tanks, and the other, the Euro doesn't tank.

Let's assume the first: the Euro tanks.

On the day you took out the contract, the USD–EUR exchange rate was 1.30 – 1. That is, \$1.30 for €1. Thus, if the company receives €1,000 this would equal \$769.23. If the Euro tanks and the exchange rate levels off, then you might reach parity between the US Dollar and the Euro at a 1-for-1 exchange. In this case, the US-based company wins as they receive more Dollars for each Euro it receives. This would be a positive outcome for the company.

Let's take a look at the second scenario: the Euro doesn't tank, in fact, it gains in value.

Since we are discussing the possibility of Brexit, it could be that the Pound Sterling tanks and UK investor drop the Pound like hot coal and jump into the Euro. Under this scenario, the value of the Euro would skyrocket. This is the scenario your company was worried about.

So, your company took out the options contract hoping that it would be covered should the worst happen. For the sake of illustration, let's assume that the USD-EUR exchange rate goes to $2 for €1. In this case, €1,000 suddenly becomes $500.

As you can see, this scenario is about a bad as it could get. It would not only represent a serious loss in terms of USD, but there is no guarantee that it could actually be the exchange; after all, it could jump to $2.50 for €1. With exchange rates, you never know how it could play out.

So, your company gets its local bank to underwrite the contract setting the exchange at $1.45 for €1 since you figure you can deal with the drop of 15 points on the Dollar, but not more. The bank is happy to underwrite at that rate because they figure they wouldn't lose money on the deal. In the worst of cases, they dump a bunch of Dollars and keep the more valuable Euros.

In the event that the Euro tanks, you won't need the contract. Your bank will thank you for your business and charge you a flat processing fee simply for underwriting the contract. Basically, it's just to cover whatever was paid to the underwriters for drafting up the contract.

But, let's assume that the Euro doesn't tank and it shoots up to the moon. Let's consider the Euro going to $2.50 for €1. In that case, you thank your lucky stars that you had that option. It kicks into gear, the bank pays out the exchange rate at $1.45 for €1 and you don't take a serious hit. In addition, the bank will charge you 1% on the total of the transaction to cover its administrative expenses.

In this example, you engaged in a derivatives contract since the contract itself was only to agree on a price for the currency to be exchanged. You didn't sign a contract for the currency itself. That is a separate transaction that is governed by a different contract.

At the end of the day, you are betting on something happening, or not. That is what derivatives are all about. Banks act like bookies in which they take in a bunch of bets, let things play out, and then collect when the bets are done.

It should also be said that this type of transaction is highly risky for all those involved as there could be any number of factors involved in the deal. So, if something should go wrong, it will go wrong for a lot of people... and really fast.

Options Basics

So now that we have a better understanding of what options are and how it essentially works, it should be noted that this currency transaction is only one example of the type of options contracts which you can become involved in.

Consequently, you need to be aware of the different types of transactions that may happen at any given time. It is up to the managers of a company to understand the risks the company is exposed to and how options can be used to hedge their position.

Often, you will hear the word "hedge" being used to refer to protecting your position against potential risks that may arise from uncertain conditions in the economy, political situations, or even disruptions in the supply of commodities such as oil and gas.

On the surface, there are different types of options such as Exchange Traded Funds (ETFs), which are very popular with commodities such as oil and gas, futures contracts, again very popular with commodities, equities, bonds, and currency, among others.

These types of contracts, as I have mentioned, do not represent the actual underlying asset in any way. You are not actually purchasing an asset unless you engage in a contract such as futures contracts in which you are locking in today's price for tomorrow's production of a specific commodity.

Although you need to be aware as not all futures contracts will specific physical delivery of the commodity. For instance, oil futures lock in a price today for the oil production that will be delivered three months from now. But I am not an oil refinery. So, I don't have any need for the actual physical oil. So, what I can do is let the contract mature. When I am ready to take physical delivery, I can turn around and sell the same oil at a different price, hopefully higher, to a company which actually needs to the oil to produce their products.

This example underscores how you need to be aware if the contract actually stipulates physical delivery. As with most ETFs, you will not get physical delivery of the underlying asset. What you will get is a check for the price of that asset. It is debatable whether the asset itself is more valuable than the cash. However, there are many scenarios in which cash would be worthless and the commodities would be king.

While that's a topic for another day, it's worth noting that options can help you hedge against the worst case scenario situations you have identified as part of your forecasting. As an investor, it could be a chance to capitalize on potential market fluctuations.

The Mechanics of Options

In essence, options are underwritten by financial institutions that are duly registered and supervised by the Securities and Exchange Commission (SEC) and are subject to a series of financial and banking regulations. The SEC is in charge of making sure that no monkey business is going and that all financial institutions comply with the regulations set forth in applicable legislations.

That being said, options are contracts between two parties (though it is possible for multiple parties to become involved) which agree on the price, term, assets, and other conditions that will trigger the contract.

Since the essence of an option is that it is optional, and thereby not forcing the parties to follow through, there are ground rules that govern the actual process of the contract.

For instance, there may be *force majeure* clauses which would void the contract in case of a serious and unexpected event such as a terrorist attack, natural disaster, or some other unforeseen event. These clauses can be included as provisions to protect the parties involved.

Beyond that, there are standard clauses that stipulate that the parties may withdraw from the contract prior 48-hour notice, or the parties might have to pay a certain amount of money for withdrawing from the contract altogether.

The fact of the matter is that each contract is different and contemplates different circumstances as provided for in the text itself. Once the contract is approved and signed, it is notarized and registered with the SEC. This gives the contract public faith.

If, and when, the contract is enacted, the parties must follow through on what is agreed, and everyone goes home happy. If the contract is not enacted, then the deal is off the table and everyone walks away.

Call Options

The first of the two general types of options we are going to be talking about are the "call options".

In short, a call gives the holder of the contract the right to buy the underlying asset but does not have the obligation to do so.

Now, let's break down this definition further.

First of all, call options are put into place when an investor is looking to purchase at a specified price. In that case, you could be tracking the price of any security, derivative, or basically any type of financial instrument.

So, when an investor decides to put this option in, the stock broker will become aware of this intention and inform the investor that the asset has fallen to the desired price. When this happens, the call option can be enacted, and the purchase goes through.

In the days of manual trading in which most orders were phoned in, investors and brokers usually had standing agreements. They would execute the options by phone and then sign the paperwork after the fact just so they could have legal backing.

With the advent of electronic trading, brokers and investors don't need to phone in their options. They can pre-program their electronic trading software and make the deal. This makes trading a lot faster and it allows for a greater number of transactions to be carried out in a single day.

But there's a catch—when traders put in their call options, they will set them at a specific price. So, when that security falls to that price, the buy order is immediately generated, and the security is sold. No questions asked. This is done because the option had already been set up that way.

Of course, the trader could kill the option if they feel the price will rebound. But it's important to note that if you are going to be exercising options, then you need to be at the wheel the whole time. If you do fall asleep at the wheel, then you might find yourself in a tough spot.

Put Options

Put options are the opposite of call options. These options give the holder the right to sell but not the obligation to do so.

Again, both investors and brokers will have standing agreements as part of the business they do. If an investor hires a professional portfolio manager, then the manager will have *carte blanche* to do as they see fit. This means that the need to call in orders is not needed.

Just like call options, put options can be programmed through electronic trading platforms, either run by individual investors or portfolio managers. The sell order is triggered when the underlying asset reaches a specific price. Of course, orders can be canceled, but the broker needs to be ready to do so.

Let's look at a practical example that will illustrate how both types of options work.

Let's assume that the underlying asset is a stock. The asset is "X" number of shares for ABC Company. The current share price for ABC Company is $10 per share. Since this is a solid company, investors are interested in purchasing more stock. However, the current sale price is a bit too high for their liking. So, a call option is placed for this stock. The buy order will be triggered when the asset reaches $9 per share.

So, let's assume that it does. The buy order is triggered for 100 shares at $9 apiece. Voila! The trade has been made.

Conversely, those who are holding the shares of ABC Company have decided they are willing to share if the price jumps to $11 per share. When this happens, the sell order is automatically triggered, and the stock is sold.

As such, let's say that it does happen. The share price of ABC jumps to $11. Consequently, the sell order is executed, and the sale goes through.

In this example, the investors who want to buy are waiting for the price of the stock to fall to a point where they feel comfortable. In contrast, the holders of the stock are willing to sell, if and when, the stock reaches a level they too feel comfortable with.

This example works with round figures for the sake of simplicity. In the real world, share prices often have a trading range of a few cents per share. However, when you multiply a few cents over a few thousand shares, then you are making sizeable income on every trade.

Options contracts

As I mentioned earlier, options are contracts. Despite the fact that they are legally binding, thus meaning you could get sued over breach of contract, you are not obligated to go through with the sale or purchase of the underlying asset.

The reason for this is that investors wanted to give themselves some leeway in case circumstance changed unexpectedly. And believe me, they do change in a hurry. So the best thing to keep in mind is that an option is there to protect you from any possible negative outcomes. However, you must be ready to act in case something goes wrong.

Valuation of Options

This is the tricky part.

Valuation of the derivatives market is largely a guessing game. Most statistical models used to value derivatives are mainly statistical models that factor in trading averages and other input factors such time, supply of the asset, inflation, exchange rates, and well, you can imagine that some of these models get pretty complex.

However, the basic element which determines the valuation of assets and options is supply and demand. When a security or commodity is under intense pressure from a lack of supply, prices will skyrocket as investors seek to lock in their prices before they reach the moon.

This usually triggers a healthy number of options, both call and put, since everyone is looking to get a good deal. Those that hold the security or commodity would like to sell when the price is at its highest point, while buyers will be looking to get in before the price of the security or commodity reaches its peak.

At this point, electronic trading can wreak havoc on the price of an asset since the market can be flooded in a matter of minutes with sell orders and kill the price of the asset, or become inundated with buy order and push the price up through the roof.

For most investors, valuing options is about making bets and having the cash and credit to cover them in case they lose. So, it pays to do your homework and make sure that whatever happens, you are ready to make the call, or kill the deal before it happens.

Please bear in mind that the valuation of derivatives is based largely on suppositions about what could, or could not happen. As such, it's important to consider the circumstances which you might be facing ahead of making a decision.

Since there is really no way to predict how high, or how low, the price of an asset will go, then you must be aware to make deals happen at the right time. I encourage folks to sell when they feel they are comfortable with the profit they are going to make, and buy at a point where they feel they are going to make money on the upswing.

Your best bet is to become familiar with market averages. There is the two-day market average, 10-day, 50-day, and 200-day averages. Of course, there are others such as one-year, two-year, five-year, or even longer averages. But those types of averages serve better as historical data rather than data that will be used to base trading decisions.

Therefore, you must become familiar with these averages so that you can get a sense of where prices are tending (either upward or downward). Don't be fooled by sudden spikes or drops. These fluctuations are a normal part of trading. Unless you are a day trader, short-term effects should have no bearing on the overall trend you are seeing in the data.

Now, if you are involved in highly-speculative short-term trading, then the two-day average is the one you want to look at. But if you are in it for the long haul, then longer data sets will help you improve your decision-making abilities.

Summary

In this chapter, we went over options. We stated that options are contracts which give the holder the right to buy or sell, but not the obligation to do so.

The valuation of options, despite the use of complex statistical modeling, is largely based on supply and demand. As such, if you are familiar with the trends in the price of the securities or commodities you are looking to trade, then you can be sure that you are going to make considerable gains.

Otherwise, you had better consider the option of hiring a professional portfolio manager who can make the best investment decisions for you. At the end of the day, doing your homework is essential in determining what the best course of action may be for you and for your portfolio.

I would highly advise you to seek professional advice before putting your money into place. Consequently, you will put yourself in a position to be successful while managing your risk as best as you possibly can.

Finally, it pays to become familiar with technical analysis, that is, the use of quantitative data that can allow you to make informed decisions based on the data sets available, especially if there are healthy sets of historical data available.

So, please bear in mind that research is one of the core elements to any successful trader. Be aware of falling asleep at the wheel as this may cause you to lose control of the ship and hit an iceberg that's hidden somewhere underneath the water.

Chapter 2: Different Types of Options

In the previous chapter, we went over the general guidelines as to what options are. We drilled down into how options can be used. In addition, we discussed a sample exercise that will allow you to better understand how options work in the financial world.

In this chapter, we will focus on the different types of options contracts and how these may vary according to the different provisions that are included in their drafting. This implies that there is a myriad of options in addition to the standard call and put options.

Various Options Markets

It is important to note that options are not exclusive to one market or one country. Options are a worldwide phenomenon, though the laws and regulations to these contracts do vary from country to country.

As such, investors based in the United States will have to comply with the rules and regulations set forth by the SEC. This is a different situation in Europe as each country sets forth a different set of regulations governing the issuance of options trades.

In a nutshell, it boils down to the individual brokerage firms that handle this type of transactions. So, large multinational banks are governed by the laws of the country in which they are based, and if conducting operations overseas, they are also governed by applicable international banking regulations such as BASILEA, and the local laws of the other party's home country.

As you can see, this is a complex endeavor since there are applicable laws from all parts of the world and not just one, host country. At the end of the day, it pays for both investors and brokers to do their due diligence in order to avoid potential legal complications.

One other consideration on the various options markets, many of the transactions conducted in the derivatives market are usually insured by a secondary insurance company that provides coverage to large deals. Often, these insurance companies also have a multinational presence. Therefore, these insurance firms must also comply with applicable legislation.

In order to simplify contracts, the contract may stipulate that the contract itself is governed by the laws of a specific nation. In which case, any disputes and issues must be resolved in the jurisdiction indicated in the contract itself. However, the laws of each individual nation still apply especially in case there is any criminal wrongdoing which may lead to indictments. Of course, this is a bit of an extreme case, but it serves to highlight the legal ramifications of these types of deals.

Different Types of Options Contracts

So, let's take a look at the different types of options contracts out there in the market today.

Call options

As discussed earlier, these are contracts which trigger a purchase order at a specified price.

Put options

Also, these contracts triggers sell orders when an asset reaches a specified price. There are two interesting variations on this type of contract.

The so-called "stop-loss" order is used when the price of an asset falls below the break-even point for a particular deal. In this case, the investor decides how much they are willing to lose before making a deal to sell. In this case, the reason for holding on to a stock despite it losing money is due to the hope of it bouncing back.

The other variation is the "minimum gain", that is, the least that you are willing to accept as a profit. So, you will not sell unless the asset reaches a certain price. Even if you are making money on the deal, the holder of the security is prepared to forego this profit unless the asset reaches the specified price in the option.

American style

No, we're not talking about hamburgers here.

An American style contract offers a good deal of flexibility, especially in terms of a contract's expiration date. American-style contracts allow for deals to be made ahead of the contract's expiration or right at the expiration. This offers much greater flexibility as investors don't necessarily have to wait for the asset's price to reach a certain point or wait until the contract is up.

European style

This is a much more restrictive contract. Typically, European-style contracts do not allow for trades to be made ahead of the contract's expiration or at different price points than the agreed one.

This type of contract offers more security in terms of having clear rules and provisions, though it does make transaction somewhat riskier if there are no *force majeure* clauses included.

Exchange traded options

These contracts are those which are listed in public stock exchanges such as the New York Stock Exchange or the Chicago Stock Exchange. As their name suggests, these options are public. So, anyone can buy into them, and cash out at any time. These options must be conducted through a duly registered and supervised broker.

Unlike private options trades, in which any parties can engage in them, publicly traded options must comply with the rule and regulations of the land.

The most famous of these types of contracts is the Exchange Traded Funds (ETFs) mentioned earlier. ETFs usually have an underlying asset, a commodity, which can be bought into by any investor who chooses to invest in that fund.

These funds are offered by duly registered and supervised financial entities and are managed by professional money managers. Since these managers are sworn to uphold their fiduciary obligation, they will do their best to protect their investor's money. Otherwise, they could be disbarred, face severe penalties, and even incarceration.

ETFs are good investment vehicles for those who want exposure to commodities with the means to diversify their portfolio but are not actually interested in physical delivery of the underlying asset. A good example of this is an oil ETF. Unless you want barrels of oil showing up at your doorsteps, you're better off just collecting a check for your winnings.

Options Classified by Underlying Asset

Thus far, we have talked about underlying assets in options contracts. So, let's take a look at the different types of underlying assets.

- **Stock options** – This option holds the underlying asset as stock in publicly traded companies.

- **Index options** – These are basically the same as a stock option, except that these options track a stock index such as the Dow Jones or Nasdaq. As such, the underlying asset is the stock of a group of companies rather than one, individual company.

- **FOREX** – These are options in the currency market. These could be like the first example we provided in the introduction of this book, or it could be directly in the currency exchange market. This is a highly speculative and risky market. It is definitely not for beginners nor the faint of heart.

- **Futures contracts** – This type of option enables investors to lock in the price of a commodity at present while taking delivery of such commodities at a later date. This is ideal when price fluctuations are taken into account. Futures also apply to currencies.

- **Commodity options** – The commodities involved in this type of contract can be any type of commodity so long as there is a mechanism which can set the price fairly.

- **Basket options** – In this case, the underlying asset is not just one, or one type of asset. Rather, it can be several assets including commodities, stocks, and bonds. These types of investment vehicles are created with the intent to hedge risk through diversification.

Options by Date of Expiration

In this type of contract, options are classified by their date of expiration and not by price or any other provisions contained in the contract. This means that the contract will only be enacted so long as the term is met.

It's worth noting that contracts do not follow a template that is set in stone, but rather, they follow general guidelines which provide their structure.

As such, options contracts by date have the following characteristics:

- **Regular options**. These contracts generally last 30 days unless otherwise stated. This tends to be the default term on options contracts, though provisions can be included to address specific terms or extensions given market conditions and so on.

- **Weekly options**. Just as its name indicates, weekly options have a 7-day term attached to them. These are ideal for investors who are trading in the short term. Also, these options are a staple of high-frequency trading in which many trades are conducted on a regular basis.

- **Quarterly options**. These contracts have an expiration date attached to a quarter, that is, a three-month period. These are more common with longer-term traders and investors. This type of option provides more flexibility when tracking the price of a security or a commodity during a longer period of time.

- **Long-term Expiration Anticipation Securities**. Also known as LEAPS, they are available for a wide array of securities over a much longer term. LEAPS can be bought at any time in the year but always expire in January. They can be bought for periods of up to three years.

- **Employee stock options.** These types of contracts are offered in lieu of increased monetary compensation or as an incentive for employees to become more committed in the company. These are called options because employees have the choice to hold or sell their stake in the company's equity. Since the financial scandals that rocked the financial industry in the early 2000s, employee stock options have been heavily regulated.

- **Cash settled options.** In this type of contract, the parties may choose to settle the transaction of the underlying asset with cash instead of the asset itself. This is common with ETFs. It's important to read the fine print with ETFs as there may be specific provisions that commodities included as underlying assets may be "unallocated" which means that the holder will never receive the actual, physical asset, but rather, its equivalent in cash.

- **Exotic options.** With these contracts, there are specific provisions that are made to them which may include complex stipulations.

Therefore, there are a wide variety of exotic contracts. These are also known as Non-Standardized options in which they contain specific provisions that adjust to specific markets.

- **Barrier options**. For these contracts, the holder is paid if the underlying asset reaches a specific price, or not. This is very similar to the traditional call and put option with the difference that the transaction will be triggered as soon as the underlying security or commodity reaches the agreed price or not, hence, the difference. With traditional calls and puts, the sell or buy order is placed when the actual price triggers it.

- **Binary options**. This contract contemplates a payout to the holder if, and when, the contract expires with a profit to the holder. The payout is generally in monetary terms.

- **Chooser options**. The name for this contract is derived from the fact that the holder may choose to convert the contract into a call or put at the expiration of the contract. In essence, the holder decides what is best for them at the expiration of the contract.

- **Compound options**. This is called "compound" since the underlying asset is another options contract.

- **Look Back Options**. In this case, there is no fixed price, but rather, the holder of the contract may choose the best price for the underlying asset as seen throughout the term of the contract. This is frequently used with currencies.

Benefits of Options

Options offer a series of benefits to their holders. But also, options provide mutual benefit to all parties involved so long as all sides are able to adequately manage risk and understand the valuation of the underlying assets. Here are some of the main benefits of options.

1. They offer flexibility to investors and financial firms.
2. Investors can hedge risk by locking in prices through futures contracts.
3. Companies and individuals can protect themselves against fluctuations in currency prices.

4. Contracts can be negotiated based on the specific needs of all parties.
5. Contracts can be settled in cash without actually having to settle in the underlying asset.

These are the main benefits that options can provide investors. It's important to note that the underlying assets which give support to these contracts should be thoroughly researched in order to understand where potential risk may lie.

Potential Risks of Options

Risk is an inherent part of any trading done in the derivatives market. As such, it is important for investors to understand such risks. Given this condition, here are some of the most relevant risks that may affect options contracts.

1. Market volatility as seen in violent swings in asset prices.
2. Lack of supply in order to guarantee delivery of a physical asset.
3. Cases of insolvency or illiquidity on the part of investors.
4. Incorrect valuation due to a lack of understanding of the underlying asset.
5. Inappropriate term of contract due to a lack of foresight.

These risks can be remedied by a thorough understanding of the underlying assets and how these can be used to leverage these contracts. Consequently, investors need to be aware of such risk. By understanding risks and potential pitfalls, investors can ensure that they are covered in case any unforeseen events should take place.

Chapter 3: Technical Options Terminology

In this chapter, we are going to be taking a closer look at some terms and definitions related to options trading. This terminology is intended to give a quick reference guide for whenever you have any questions about any specific terms or definitions.

Therefore, it is important for you to become familiar with these terms as they commonly come up within the investment world. Also, some of these expressions have a cross-cutting appeal, as they are not exclusive to options trading, but may be found in all sorts of trading situations.

So, we're going to drill down into each one of these in alphabetical order.

Asian Option

In this type of option, the payout in the contract is dependent upon the average price of the underlying asset over a given period of time (for example, a week, or a month) as opposed to the European and American options which depend on the maturity of the contract.

Asset Swap

In a derivatives contract, two parties may choose to simply swap assets regardless of price or any other underlying factor. This type of contract is very useful in cases in which both parties are in need of acquiring one asset and are perfectly willing to part with the other. For example, both parties may switch a specific amount of currency regardless of the exchange rates.

Antedate

In legal contracts, the date is one which occurs prior to the maturity of the contract, or occurrence of the stipulations in the contract. It is also known as a "backdate".

Bear Call Spread

A bear call spread, also referred to a call credit spread, is a strategy in which an options contract is intended when there is an expected decline in the price of the underlying asset. This can be done by purchasing the option at a given strike price. Then, the asset is sold at the expiration date but at a lower price. The maximum profit which can be made is the same as the original credit received when beginning the trade.

Binary Option

In this type of option, the outcome of the option is considered upon a "yes/no" proposition and hence its binary nature. As such, the investor makes money at the expiration of the contract, then the investor is "in the money". If the investor loses money, then they are "out of the money". This contract depends solely on its expiration date and represents one large bet which could play out in one of two ways.

Breakeven Point

The breakeven point is the point in which the sale price of an underlying asset reaches its original cost. In other words, the investor makes their money back but does not make any profit on the sale of the original security or option.

Bull Call Spread

This is essentially the opposite of the bear call spread. In this option, the investor will purchase call options at a given strike price. Then, the investor will sell the options at a higher price upon the expiration date. Profit is to be made from the difference between the lower purchase price and the higher sell price.

Cash or Nothing Put

This is a type of exotic option in which there is a fixed price, often equal to the strike price, which serves to trigger the payout of the contract if the underlying asset's price falls below the strike price. Otherwise, the payout is zero.

Cash Trigger

This is the price point in which an investor has decided to trigger the buy/sell option of the contract. In this condition, the option will go through and the trade is completed.

Cash-settled Options

These options are settled in monetary terms, in the currency which is agreed upon, and not with actual physical delivery of the underlying asset. This is a common feature of ETFs.

Charm (Delta Decay)

"Charm" is the term which refers to the rate at which the delta of an option varies over time. It refers to the second order derivative of an option's valuation. This is considered as once to time and once to price. It can also be considered as a derivative of theta, the indicator which measures time decay of that option's valuation.

Contingency Order

A contingency order may be executed when specific conditions are met in an investor's portfolio. For instance, these may be executed when the investor is lacking funds and needs to sell in order to free up cash. In other cases, very specific conditions may be met in terms of depth and scope, which will trigger the option.

Contract Market

This is a board of trade, or an exchange, that has been designated to the trade of any given options or futures. These must be duly registered with its corresponding supervisory authority in the country in which it operates.

Date Certain

This term is used to refer to the exact date on which stipulated actions on a contract are to take place. As such, when the specified date is reached, the action is then executed as per the terms of the contract.

Deal Ticket

This is a record of all the term, conditions, and other pertinent information in an agreement. The deal ticket is generated after the transaction of the contracts takes place.

Delta-Gamma Hedging

This is a strategy in which both delta and gamma hedges are used in order to mitigate the risk involved with regard to the changes in an underlying asset and in the delta itself.

Early Exercise

This term refers to the execution of a buy or sell order in a contract prior to the expiration date. In this case, the contract may stipulate that the order be executed when the stipulated strike price is hit and not upon the maturity of the contract.

Exchange Traded Option

This is when individual investors may buy into a contract which is open on a publicly traded market under the strike price. The contract may be executed when either the contract matures or the strike price is hit.

Far Option

This type of option is the one with a longer expiration date contained in a calendar option spread. This option involves buying and selling options with different expiration dates. Under this model, the short spread is the nearest one in expiration while the long one has the farthest expiration date.

Extrinsic Value

This term refers to the difference in the market price of an option, also referred to as "premium" and its intrinsic value. Extrinsic value also refers to the part of an option's price which is not determined by factors pertaining to the contract's underlying asset, but rather, it is due to external factors.

Failure to Deliver

As its name suggests, this refers to when one of the parties involved in the contract does not meet their obligations. Penalties and other sanctions may be imposed as per the stipulations of the contract. In general, this is due when one party may not have the money to cover their position or the other is unable to deliver on the underlying asset.

Fiduciary Call

In a fiduciary call, parties use the option in order to execute a cost-effective strategy to limit the costs associated with the exercise of a call option. Consequently, when an investor exercises a call option, the investor must have the necessary funds to make the call when the time comes to make the purchase.

Floating Price

A floating price refers to a price which is not fixed, but rather, may fluctuate according to market conditions. This type of price is intended to address variations in market prices such as in commodities like oil and gas. This may also apply to exchange rates in the case of currency transactions.

Gamma

A gamma refers to the rate of change in an option's delta valuation. It refers to a one-point move in the underlying asset's price. Therefore, a dealt hedge is used to reduce the gamma in an option, so the option's price is maintained over time.

Illiquid Option

This is a contract which cannot be easily sold or transferred into cash in a short period of time in terms of the current market. This could be due to a number of factors. In essence, an option may be illiquid if the yield on the options are too low, or if there are stipulations in the contract which make it difficult to keep.

Lambda

This term refers to the ratio of change in the monetary price, usually in Dollars, of an option. It refers to the 1% change in the expected price volatility or implied volatility of the underlying asset. The lambda can be used to tell investors how much the price of an option will change given the changes in the implied volatility of the option's price.

Married Put

A married put is essentially an insurance policy for investors. This is a strategy in which an investor, who holds a long position, purchases an option known as "at the money" on the same asset, in order to protect themselves against the depreciation of the same asset's price.

Max Pain

This is the strike price of an underlying asset in an option that would cause financial loss to the investor in either a call or put option. Upon reaching their max pain point, investors may choose to get out of a contract and cut their losses.

Natural Hedge

This is a protection strategy which is used by investors and companies in order to protect themselves from currency fluctuations. For instance, they may choose to move operations to another country, or do business in a different currency, in order to avoid potential losses due to exchange rate volatility.

Non-Equity Option

These contracts refer to those which have assets other than securities as underlying assets. These assets could be currencies or commodities.

Omega

This Greek refers to the measurement of various characteristics of options. In particular, it measures the change of the underlying asset's price as compared to the price of the option itself.

One-touch Option

This type of contract pays a premium on the contract itself if the underlying's asset's market price reaches a specified point.

Outright Option

This refers to options which are bought and sold individually. In essence, this refers to any type of option bought and sold privately. This could be done between a bank and an investor. It is the basic type of option on an underlying asset. It can be either a call or put.

Over the Counter Market

Over the counter markets or OTC markets are those which do not have a specific physical location such as a given stock exchange. OTC markets can be traded by phone or email in which financial institutions trade with investors.

Perpetual Option

This is an exotic option which stipulates no maturity or time limit. The actual lifespan of a perpetual option may range from a few days to years. Its expiration is triggered by specific conditions such as the market price of the underlying asset. These options are agreed upon the parties based on their needs or expectations.

Physical Options

In this type of options contract, the underlying asset is a physical one in which the investors choose to take physical allocation of such underlying asset. With these contracts, investors may turn around and sell the physical asset or roll the option over.

Ratio Spread

This type of spread measures the ratio between long and short positions, that is, the number ratio of short positions as compared to the long ones. Typically, short positions will outnumber long ones 2 to 1.

Rolling Options

These contracts offer the investor the option to take the payout of the contract upon maturity or have extended the expiration of the contract thereby rolling it over. This allows investors to have flexibility both in term and market price. These options are preferred by investors who are feeling bullish on the price of the underlying asset.

Russian Option

Russian options generally do not have an expiration date and give the holder the option to sell at the best price during the lifespan of the contract. These are considered perpetual options and due to their nature, are also considered exotic options.

Spot Price

This term refers to the current price of an asset. It is the average of buy and sell prices over a given period of time. Spot price may also serve to determine the trigger in a contract.

Strike Price

The strike price is the price in which a contract can be exercised. The strike price can be different from the spot price of a security or commodity. In any event, the contract may stipulate the strike price when a specified spot price is reached.

Theta

This is another of the Greeks. In essence, theta measures the decline in the value of an option over a given period of time. Even if all factors remain constant, a contract still loses value over time as the contract draws closer to its maturity.

Time Decay

This term refers to the change in an option over a given period of time, generally, the maturity of the contract itself. Over time, options lose value for the sake of being open. This implies that the longer an option is open, the longer it loses value.

Uncovered Option

This term refers to options in which the investor buys into an option without holding a counter position. The investor may not hold a long position in the underlying asset or have the cash to cover the position. This is called a naked position. It is highly risky and may lead to insolvency on the part of the investor.

Underlying Asset

This is the asset, a security, bond, commodity, or any other asset, which serves as the support for the contract itself. This may be a physical asset or an intangible asset. Options may stipulate delivery of the underlying asset or may be settled in cash.

Vega

This is the measurement of the price sensitivity of the underlying asset of an options contract. Vega measures a 1% in the implied volatility of the underlying asset.

Wasting Asset

This refers to a depreciating asset that loses value over time even if it is not used. This is a type of fixed asset such as vehicles or machinery.

Zomma

Another of the Greek options. Zomma measures the change in gamma in relation to the changes in the volatility of an underlying asset.

These terms are some of the various terms you will come across throughout your journey into options trading. In particular, we have introduced the Greek terms which are associated with options trading. We will discuss these terms, their calculations in depth in a later chapter.

For now, I would encourage you to become familiar with these terms. Your understanding of these terms will help you become more proficient in your mastery of the options trading domain. So, it would certainly pay for you to do your homework as a part of your daily trading routine.

Chapter 4: Options Trading vs. Stock Trading

In this chapter, we are going to take a closer look at how securities trading differs from trading options. In particular, stocks, which are the most popular form of securities, are traded openly through various markets and means.

As such, most investors are familiar with stock trading but may not be too familiar at how options can be used, both in the equities market and on its own as a part of a broader investment strategy. Thus, it's imperative that investors become familiar with the various alternatives which are available to them as part of an overall investment strategy.

One other point that I would like to make is that diversification is a fundamental strategy which looks to hedge risk by spreading investable assets over various investment classes. Naturally, options are one type of investment class which investors can take advantage of.

It's also important to note that securities and options, while usually related to each other, are traded in different markets.

Since securities refer to stock of publicly traded companies, they are traded in primary markets in which they are presented to the investment public through financial firms which broker the trades of these stocks.

Consequently, investors work in tandem with these investment firms in order to buy and sell securities, either as individual purchases of stocks or through other investment vehicles such as mutual funds. Thus, investors have various ways in which they can gain exposure to the stock market.

Options are involved in the securities market, though they are not securities in themselves. As we have started earlier, options are considered derivatives since they don't trade assets as such. Instead, the options use assets as support for the contract itself.

This is why the term "underlying" asset is so commonly used when referring to options. Of course, a futures contract may ultimately lead to the purchase or sale of an asset. However, the option itself does not deal with the asset in question.

Since there is a myriad of options available, investors must be well aware of the choices they have available to them. The more investors become familiar with options, the better they will come to understand the opportunities that are available to them.

It should be noted that options trading is not for beginners and does require a certain level of proficiency. While you may not need to hold a Ph.D. in finance and economics to trade in options, it is worthwhile to take the time to study in order to truly comprehend what is behind this type of financial instrument.

In addition, I would encourage you to seek professional financial advice while you become proficient in your trading skills. That way, you can compare your understanding of financial instruments and investments with that of licensed professionals. In fact, the worst thing that could happen is you pay a professional for a few hours of their time, but you end up learning about financial markets from experts who have experience in the game.

Overview of Equities Trading

So, let's take a look at how equities trading actually work.

In this discussion, we are going to focus solely on equities. We are not going to be discussing bonds or commodities as we are being explicit about comparing equities and options. This is an important distinction I would like to make since bonds and commodities, while falling under the securities umbrella, are completely different types of investments and have their own nuances. As such, discussing them implies an entirely different subject.

Thus, equities are the stock of publicly traded companies. A company "goes public" when it files to be listed on one of the stock exchanges located in their home country of operation. This is important to note since there are stock exchanges all over the world.

For instance, virtually every developed nation in the world has its own stock market in which publicly traded companies are listed. This is a fundamental requirement as company stock may not be traded without going through an exchange unless there is a specific contract offering individual investors direct sales of stock.

Now, for the sake of simplicity, we are going to use the United States as an example. However, if you are interested in trading in other countries, I would highly encourage you to read up on that particular market's laws and regulations as they may vary from country to country.

That being said, there are several stock exchanges throughout the United States. The most popular stock exchange is the New York Stock Exchange. This is the physical building in which stocks are traded. You may have seen the famous trading floor scenes in Hollywood films and television shows.

Now, there are two major players in all stock markets. There are the investors, and there are the investment firms which broker the sale of stock to the investing public. This is needed due to the regulations in US law which stipulates that licensed brokers are the ones who must facilitate the purchase and sale of publicly traded stock.

The reason for this is that there are several regulations which supervise the actions carried out by players in financial markets. As such, the law restricts the ways in which publicly traded companies may sell their stock to private investors.

It's worth mentioning that this applies to publicly traded companies since private companies, those which are not traded on any stock exchange, are free to do as they see fit with their company's stock.

When a private company chooses to go public, it must do so through a duly registered investment firm. Typically, these investment firms are large banks which deal with these types of transactions. The investment firm then underwrites the Initial Public Offering (IPO) of this company.

In an IPO, a private company, which will go public for the first time ever, will place their shares on sale to the investing public. The investment firm will then set a share price based on what they believe will be the best price investors will pay.

Now, depending on the company going public, investors may line up to get their hands on the IPO. Of course, the firm that's underwriting the IPO will have its own customers who will most likely get first dibs on the IPO.

Once the paperwork is completed and the IPO gets the green light, the newly traded company will hit the trading floor. At this point, the first wave of investors that gets their hands on the IPO must pony up the cash for the sale of the stock.

Then, the first wave of investors may choose to sell at any time they see fit. If the company is a hot-ticket item, they may choose to hold on a bit while the price goes up. When this happens, the investors that got into the IPO will clean up. The reason for this is that the investors who get into the IPO will pay a much lower price than what the market may be willing to pay.

After a company's IPO, they will be traded as part of the usual operations on a stock exchange. And consequently, are subject to options contracts as investors begin to consider this newly-listed corporation as an investment choice.

Valuation of Stocks

One of the most common questions in stock trading is the valuation of stocks.

The valuation of stocks is a highly psychological and emotional situation as investors may lose their cool and overpay for a stock that's "hot" while there may be companies whose stock is absolutely worthless.

In essence, stock prices are quoted as individual share prices, that is, the price of a single share of a publicly traded company. Your average, run-of-the-mill publicly traded corporation may have millions of outstanding shares which make up its share capital. In this case, the price of an individual share may be multiplied by the millions of outstanding shares thus arriving at its total share capital.

The individual share price is essentially determined by supply and demand. When a stock is hot, but there is a limited supply of shares available, then the price will go up as investors are willing to pay more and more for each share.

On the contrary, if there is little demand for a given stock, prices will fall as sellers need to lower their price to a point where they can entice other investors to buy. The reasons for a stock price to fall may vary, but in general, they are a sign that something is not sitting well with investors.

Therefore, the price that you see quoted on the nightly news is the result of the average between the buy and sell prices that investors are paying. As such, you may not necessarily get the price that you see quoted. It could be that you might get a lower price, but you must also note that you might get a higher price, as well.

The Role of the Stockbroker

The stockbroker is the individual who conducts the transactions on the equities market. This is the person whose name appears on the file for each individual trade. Brokers will charge a commission on each trade that they make.

This commission may range from a few cents on the Dollar (this is true of high-frequency trading) to a few Dollars per trade. So, commissions can add up when you conduct a large number of trades.

Also, brokers make money when deals make money. This is the case of mutual funds. For instance, a mutual fund is an amount of money pooled from different investors. All of the investors in the pool receive a return on their money. So, let's assume the return is 3% annually. The investor will make 3% on their money. It is now the job of the broker, or portfolio manager, to make over 3% in order to make more money for themselves.

This last point illustrates how brokers can become aggressive when looking to make more money for their investments. In addition, individual brokers and firms will look to pay as little as they can in order to maximize their own profits.

Investing in Stocks

It should be said that stock trading is not for everyone.

Most folks who would like to get exposure into the stock market may choose to purchase mutual funds from their local bank, or perhaps buy into their own company's stock option plan. In such cases, funds are managed by professional money managers who have experience and knowledge in the field. With these money or portfolio, managers might make mistakes from time to time, they generally make money most of the time.

This approach is generally what most folks go for as they may not have the time nor the expertise to engage in stock trading themselves. Nevertheless, it's important for you to become familiar with the way the stock market works as you will have an understanding of how your stock portfolio is performing given the conditions of the market.

Furthermore, a solid understanding of the investment options available to you will help you determine if the advice you are getting from a portfolio manager is really the best option that is available to you, or if there are other options that have not been considered. So, as always, it pays to do your homework.

Long Term versus Short Term

One of the other considerations that investors must keep in mind is if they are looking to engage in short-term trading or long-term trading.

A general rule of thumb is that the younger the investor, the longer they have to ride out the fluctuations in the markets. So, if an investor starts out in their 20s, they will have about 24 to 40 years of investing time before they plan to retire. So, if the markets have a couple of down years here and there, it won't derail their investments barring an unprecedented collapse.

On the other hand, older investors, say in their 40s or even 50s, may choose to engage in riskier trading strategies as they need to make up for lost time. In this scenario, a long-term approach means that you won't be engaging in quite as many trades as you would if you were looking to invest in the short term. Therefore, short-term investors generally make more trades than long-term investors do.

My advice to folks who are starting out in the investment world is to think about why you are looking to invest in the first place. So, if you are simply looking to get rich, then you might consider a short-term strategy, such as day trading in order to find the best way of making a good chunk of money.

Conversely, if you are thinking about investing for retirement, then you might look into a long-term approach in which you are more risk-averse and looking to keep your money invested longer so that you can maximize your returns over the long-term.

You will get rich with either strategy. The big difference is the time in between and the risk involved. While long-term investing espouses a slowly but surely approach, short-term trading espouses a much more aggressive approach which may open you up to more risk. As such, risk might imply that you could lose your shirt in a bad deal.

So, I would advise you to sit down and go over your goals. Whatever they are, this book will surely help you arrive at a good conclusion as to how you can use options trading to help you achieve your financial goals.

Benefits of Trading Equities

When you are looking to gain exposure into the equities market, it essentially boils down to risk. Since there is a myriad of options in which you can start off with a small amount of money, you don't need to be a wealthy millionaire to get into the stock market. But you do have to be aware of how risk can play out in the equities market.

As such, trading in equities is one of the safest ways in which you can invest your money. Sure, there is always risk involved in any type of deal. And as long as you don't have a maverick portfolio manager, your money should be safe.

For investors who are looking to gain exposure to the stock market but may be more risk-averse, there are several options available.

First, there are mutual funds. As I have stated before, a mutual fund is essentially a pool of money collected from different investors. This pool of money is then taken by the investment firm that sells it and assigned to a professional portfolio or money manager. This manager will then allocate the money into the various investment vehicles that are available.

When you look into purchasing a mutual fund, there are various types.

For example, you might buy into a mutual fund that is solely invested in stocks. This fund may be focused on a general basket of stocks such as blue-chip companies like IBM, Apple, Microsoft, and so on, or perhaps on industrial companies in the areas of steel and automobiles.

Also, mutual funds may be traded as index funds. These funds track specific stock indices such as the Dow Jones or the Nasdaq. In short, a stock index is a basket of companies which are grouped together and tracked as a whole. That means that the companies in that stock index represent a group thus providing a point of reference in the performance of these companies.

The Dow Jones, for example, groups the 30 largest companies in the United States. So, an index fund that is attached to the Dow would depend on the overall performance of the Dow. This means that if the Dow is up, the fund makes money. If the Dow is down, then the fund may lose money. As such, index funds may provide a great opportunity to make money in stocks without engaging in any risky practices.

Another advantage of trading equities is that there is a myriad of investment vehicles which you can select in order to get started. That means that you don't need to have millions of dollars to get started. There are mutual funds and other investment accounts in which you can get started with as little as $100 and then make monthly contributions to the account. This is a great way for you to gain exposure into stocks without actually having to invest a large lump sum of cash.

In addition, there are other safer investments vehicles such as certificates of deposit in which investor essentially deposit money into a bank account. Then, the bank issues a certificate to which the investor has the right to collect at its maturity.

In this type of investment vehicle, the investor doesn't need to do much except check up on their monthly statement. This allows investors to have a safer investment option though the returns may not be as high as other riskier options.

Finally, it's important to note that equities allow for a high degree of flexibility and diversification. So, if you are looking to gain exposure to a wide range of companies, industries, and sectors, equities can provide you with solid investment opportunities. A good diversification strategy can help you hedge risk while considering decent returns based on market expectations.

Drawbacks of Trading Equities

By far, the biggest drawback of trading in equities is the risk of volatility.

Volatility means that there is a risk of wild fluctuations in the prices of individual stocks or major stock indices. While having a diversified strategy would limit your overall risk, there is always the possibility that one company you have invested in takes a beating, or the overall economy begins to slow down.

That is why the term "recession" is a boogeyman term that scares the living daylights out of most investors. Recessions imply a bear market, which in turn, means that the overall markets will be down from their previous highs. Thus, investors need to be aware of the fact that they may end up taking a hit in their investments or even losing money. While the prospect of losing money is never fun, those investors who are in for the long haul may take market downturns in stride as opposed to those who are more focused on a short-term strategy.

Furthermore, novice investors will find it hard to uncover the best investment opportunities that are available to them. Naturally, finding the right opportunities is a question of time and patience. As a result, many investors simply don't have the time and the freedom to do the research that is needed in order to find solid companies out there.

You could cut corners a bit by purchasing a premium data and information package from a large investment firm. These information packages contain stats, analytics, insider information, and any other data which may help investors make informed decisions. On the whole, relying on the information published by these business intelligence units is useful, though it should not be the only sources to guide your decisions.

Hence, a lack of information is one of the biggest drawbacks in the equities market. There isn't always an abundance of information. Consequently, many investors lack the overall insight needed in order to make sound financial decisions. This elevates the level of risk and may lead to potential losses if a deal goes bad.

Nevertheless, investing in equities may not turn out to be as bad as you might think. However, I would encourage you to do your homework and stay up to date on all of the different news and information. Since we are living in the information age, it is easier now to gain access to all of the information you would need in order to guide your investment decisions.

One final note on the subject of drawbacks in the equities markets, beware of following the crows. As I stated earlier, there is a serious psychological and emotional component to investing and trading. Often, most investors will get caught up in the frenzy that may arise when a stock is "hot" or there is a great opportunity out there.

One of the axioms in trading is that if you are looking to get into a stock when it's hot, then you have already missed the boat. By the time stocks are "hot", it means that the investors who got into it at the outset are the ones who cleaned up. If you get in at the top of the wave, then you will be poised to take a hit as there is nowhere to go but down after you hit the top of the wave.

That is why it pays to do your research. Focus on the historical trends of a stock. When you see that it is significantly higher as compared to its previous low, then you might be looking at the stock being overpriced. At that point, many investors will trigger their sell points and the price of the stock will come crashing down back to its average. This is called "reverting to the mean".

Equities vs Options

So then, which is better, equities or options?

The answer to that is—it depends.

It depends on what your investment strategy is and what you are looking to achieve. So, if you are looking to put some money away for retirement and you are only concerned about saving up for the long haul, then you might not concern yourself too much with options trading. You could simply choose to buy into a mutual fund and sit back while your portfolio manager handles the dirty work.

This passive investing approach provides folks with peace of mind and assurance that they are putting their money to work. On the other hand, it doesn't provide the most attractive gains. Yet, there is always room for growth and potential to make sizeable returns over time.

Now, for more active traders, equities offer a range of alternatives from which to choose from. You can jump straight into blue-chip stocks and play it safe, or you might try to look for a hidden gem out there and try to hit a home run.

Either way, equities offer the potential for growth so long as markets don't come crashing down like they did in 1929. And even if they did, you would still have the option of finding some cheap stocks which may be poised for a rebound.

Of course, stock market crashes don't happen all that frequently (thank God), but there are market downturns which you can capitalize on. Thus, if you are looking to play the role of an active investor, you might consider day trading as an option in which you can do your best to find good deals out there and make some serious cash.

In the case of options trading, I made the point of how this is not for beginners. Options trading require investors to have some proficiency in trading before they can truly make the best of their knowledge and experience in this field.

The reason for this is that the derivatives market is highly volatile and highly speculative. So, investors need to be on their toes at all times. Otherwise, a missed opportunity could lead to taking a serious hit and losing a good chunk of change.

Also, options contracts do have a lot of legal underpinnings which most folks make not be entirely familiar with. The good thing is that once you get a good grasp of the way the contracts work, you won't have a hard time navigating the waters of the options markets. Nevertheless, it does take a bit of time and study in order to reach a point where you are comfortable with trading in options.

Furthermore, trading in options requires investors to understand the nature of the underlying assets of the contract, their pricing mechanism, and how the changes to those prices may affect the overall valuation of the contract. Consequently, a novice investor may be unfamiliar with such level of depth thereby leaving the door open to potential mistakes.

There is the possibility for investors to trade in options while maintaining a more passive role. This is generally hedge fund territory as hedge funds tend to trade in more speculative markets. In general, hedge funds are clubs of rich people who pool their money together in order to take on rather big gambles.

Hedge funds will dabble in all sorts of derivatives as these are the investment vehicles which make the most money. Therefore, hedge funds will not shy away from trading in options while enabling their investors to take on as much risk and they can bear.

Often, investors in hedge funds won't be too concerned about risk so long as they get a nice check at the end of the month.

How to Choose the Right Alternative for You

Choosing the right alternative for you boils down to your approach, be it long term or short term, and your risk tolerance.

Thus, if you have all the time in the world and are risk-averse, equities might be the best course of action for you. But, if you have more risk tolerance and don't plan on waiting for 20 years to cash in, then a more aggressive approach in the derivatives market may be the better way to go.

If you are looking to be more aggressive, then I would like to advise you to see your doctor and have your blood pressure checked out because trading in a high-risk, speculative market is not for everyone, especially those faint of heart.

So, let's consider some examples that illustrate the factors that play into making a decision on the best investment approaches.

First, let's make some assumptions.

Scenario A

In this scenario, a younger investor in their 20s is looking to get started investing money. They don't have a high-paying job and are basically starting out in life. They are simply looking to invest money while building up to buy a house, start a family, and so on. This individual investor is more risk-averse and is not keen on making any high-stakes poker bets because they are concerned with losing all their money.

So, what would be the best approach?

A safer, more diversified approach. This could be a combination of mutual funds, certificates of deposit, high-interest savings accounts, regular investment accounts, a company 401k, and government bonds.

This portfolio espouses a gradual and incremental approach as this young investor may be starting out with a couple of hundred dollars. Therefore, there isn't much they can do at the beginning of their investment career though they would have the option of building up over time.

As the investor gets older and has more money put away, they may consider more aggressive strategies such as buying into index funds or ETFs. This approach would lead to greater diversification and afford bigger returns. After 30-some-odd years of investing, the individual may be poised to have enough money put away for a comfortable retirement while having a decent quality of life.

Scenario B

In this scenario, an older investor, say in their 40s, is looking to jump into investing. They have basically paid off their house, have some money put away for their kids' college, have cars paid off, and are beginning to save up for retirement. However, saving money and having it into a mutual fund or 401k may not pay out enough for them to retirement any time soon.

So, this investor chooses to be a bit more aggressive and look for alternatives that can yield greater returns. As such, this investor may look to purchase a mortgage-backed certificate. Since this type of security is used by banks to gather funds destined for home loans, investors may find that they offer higher rates of return as opposed to the run-of-the-mill certificate of deposit. In addition, mortgage-backed certificates are generally the precursor to more speculative vehicles such as mortgage-backed securities (MBS). These MBSs were the ones that got banks in trouble back in 2008 during the sub-prime mortgage crisis. Nevertheless, those that got in on the ground floor made a killing in this type of investment vehicle.

As you can see, these are more aggressive approaches that can pay off more at the end of the day. However, you do need to be aware of what you are doing and make sure that you are not setting yourself up for a trap.

The final outcome for the investor in scenario B would be making up for lost time though there is no guarantee that this more aggressive approach may yield the results they are expecting.

Final thoughts

In this chapter, we took an extensive look at how securities can become a viable investment opportunity while options, and by extension derivatives, can provide an equally profitable opportunity though with a higher level of risk attached to them.

So, I would like to point out that it is best for you to look into all of the choices available to you so that you can make the best decision based on your personal goals when you are clear on what approach you will take.

Of course, it's always a good idea to consult with investment experts who can give you their perspective on what options are available to you. This would enable you to have realistic expectations as to what you can achieve within the timeframe you have set for yourself.

As a final thought, one of the most important traits you can exhibit as an investor is patience. While there may be the temptation to go all-in on what seems to be the deal of a lifetime, patience is what will help you stay in the game for the long haul.

So, beware of following the crowd as the crowd may be ready to fall off a cliff. As such, being smart and cautious may lead you to protect yourself a lot better than you think.

Chapter 5: Options Volatility and Greek Variables

In this chapter, we are going to drill down into the nitty-gritty of options trading and the various elements that go into the analysis of such trades.

This chapter is rooted in technical analysis, that is, the use of statistical and quantitative models to make decisions on what trade ought to be conducted and how to maximize profits. As such, technical analysis is one of the essential tools that all investors must have at their disposal.

Consequently, if investors do not have at least a basic understanding of technical analysis, they may end up making erroneous decisions due to a lack of fundamental on which to base their decisions. The most important thing to keep in mind is that as you gain more experience, you will be able to find greater value in the information and data sets provided by all the various news agencies and business intelligence units out there.

So, we will be looking at some of the most important aspects to options trading and the so-called "Greeks" that are involved in the calculation of the various operations that make up options trading.

Overview of Volatility

The first element to consider is volatility. Volatility refers to the fluctuations in the prices of assets.

As we have defined earlier, all assets, regardless of their shape, color, or size, are subject to fluctuations. Unless prices are fixed by some authority, usually the government, prices will naturally fluctuate as they become affected by market forces.

In essence, market forces boil down to supply and demand, although options don't respond the same way to market forces as equities do. Equities are a prime example of how supply and demand can affect their market price.

However, options by nature lose value over time. This is an important factor to keep in mind as the loss of value may be triggered by a depreciating underlying asset. So, the longer the option is open, the more value is lost.

Nevertheless, market volatility for options is dependent on a number of factors which don't necessarily respond to market forces in the same manner as other assets or securities.

Volatility is observed in the way prices move up and down over a period of time. These changes are tracked through averages. As such, averages provide a fairly accurate estimate of what the price of a contract or an asset is in real time.

When markets are highly volatile, there are violent swings in prices going in either direction. These violent swings may cause investors to become wary of investing in that market and decide to pull out as soon as they have a chance to do so.

When investors begin pulling out, volatility is further fueled as prices won't settle back down until they hit a trough. At that point, investors may look to get back into the market since it has hit a bottom. Nevertheless, timing the bottom of a market is very hard to do and may lead investors to lose more money before they can start to see gains.

When markets are stable, assets trade in a specific range and don't normally deviate from that range. Of course, there are peaks and valleys which may grow over time. But in general, prices remain stable thus affording investors the chance to make some positive gains even if they aren't as attractive as investors would like them to be.

Impact of Volatility on Options

Volatility is fertile ground for options.

When underlying assets in options contracts present a high degree of fluctuation, investors may seek out to purchase standard calls and puts in order to hedge their positions. As such, you might see investors purchasing calls when they feel that prices are going down and want to capitalize on a dip in the market.

On the other hand, investors may look to purchase puts when they feel the market is fluctuating and they want to get out as soon as the underlying asset hits a specific price. In this case, a given strike price, that is the price that triggers the option, can be set so that the investor can get out a specific point.

Also, volatility provides investors with the opportunity to make significant short-term gains. This can be achieved through the tried and true approach of buying low and selling high.

As volatility reaches higher levels, investors may find themselves running for cover. At this point, options underwriters may attach higher premiums to the options since market volatility may cause options underwriters to cover large margins for investors.

Consider this example:

The stock of a company is trading in a very broad range. This is due to the fact that the overall market is unstable due to mixed results from companies' quarterly earnings reports, political instability, and uncertainty in international trade.

As such, investors aren't entirely sure where to allocate their investments. So, they are pulling in and out of stocks, bonds, and so on. Now, this particular company is a large multinational player and is subject to all sorts of global conditions which may affect its overall performance.

So, investors are anticipating big news on the company's forecast for the next quarter. Since this is a large multinational player that deals with international partners, the bad outlook for the international trade market has investors worried.

Consequently, investors take out a bunch of put options on the company's stock as they anticipate bad news.

At this point, this is what is going on in the minds of investors: they are concerned that the company's earnings forecast will be lower than expected. As such, they know that as soon as news breaks, they will have to dump the stock. If and when this happens, the options which have been purchased have a strike price set as a stop-loss should the price of the stock fall below the breakeven point.

Sure enough, the news breaks and the company's earnings forecast is lower than expected. This triggers a massive selloff in that stock. The price plummets and takes a huge hit.

In this case, the investors who took out puts managed to get out before they took a sizeable hit. Those who didn't ended up going along for the ride.

Now, it's worth noting that the price of the options itself would go up in terms of the premium that investors would have had to pay in order to cover their position. This is a simple case of supply and demand.

As options underwriters see the flood in puts, they will raise the premium as they may be on the hook for a number of puts that would need to be covered at a specific point. Thus, investors may end up with having to pay a higher premium for the contract itself, that is, they will get hit with higher fees as the number of puts for that particular stock keeps climbing.

Therefore, those who got in early got a good deal, while those who got in later would end up paying the highest price.

The Black-Scholes Model

The Black-Scholes Model is used to determine the fair market value or the theoretical value of a call or put option. This model takes into account six variables which are all used as inputs in order to determine the final price of a put or call option.

The variables are:
- Volatility
- Time
- Strike price
- The type of option
- The underlying asset price
- Interest rate

When all of these variables are calculated in tandem, the result is the theoretical value of the option in question.

This model is used by options traders to purchase options which are under their calculated value and sell them at a higher price than that of the Black-Scholes Model calculation. This implies that the investor will make some money based on understanding in the option is priced below or above its theoretical value.

This model can be applied to a wide range of options such as:

- American options
- Binary options
- Cash or nothing options
- FOREX options

As such, this model offers flexibility in the way the theoretical value of an option may be calculated, thus leaving investors with the option of making investment decisions based on the results this model provides. The most important thing is that it takes volatility into account. Consequently, this helps investors determine what the best course of action would be.

Greek Strategies for Options

Throughout this book, we have talked about the Greeks. Now, we are not specifically referring to the

Greeks of lore, but rather, we are talking about a series of strategies which are named after letters in the Greek alphabet.

As such, the Greeks refer to strategies used in trading options.

In this section, we are going to take a closer look at how these Greeks work in practice.

Delta

The first of the Greeks is called "Delta".

In essence, Delta is a measure of how much the theoretical value of the option will change for every dollar the price of the underlying asset changes.

For instance, if the underlying asset is a stock which is originally valued at $10 a share, the delta of the call or put option will be the change in the options theoretical value as the price of the shares move from $10 to $11 or from $10 to $9.

The range of a Delta is from 0 to 1. Therefore, the value of a Delta will be a decimal number in that range. Also, long calls have a positive value for Delta while short calls have a negative value for Delta. Long puts have a negative Delta whereas short puts have a positive Delta.

For example, ABC Company has a price of $48, and the option has a price of $2.00 with a Delta of +0.45, and change in the price of the underlying asset, that is, from $48 to $49, will cause the options to jump to

$2.45. Conversely, if the price of the shares goes from $48 to $47, the price of the option will fall to $1.55.

As you can see in this example, the fluctuation is essentially 45 cents. In this example, we are considering the actual price of the stock and not necessarily the strike price in the option. Thus, the strike price is not taken into account, but rather, it is the asset's actual market price.

Gamma

Gamma takes the previous analysis one level deeper. So, if Delta measures the change in the price of the option as a result in the change of the price of the underlying asset, Gamma measures how much the Delta, itself, will change for every dollar in change of the underlying asset's price.

In other words, Gamma is the measure of how stable the Delta is for a given option. Thus, if there is a big move in Gamma, then the changes will be considerable in the Delta even if there is just a small move in the underlying asset´s price. Also, long calls and puts have a positive Gamma, while short puts and calls have a negative Gamma.

Let's take the data from the previous example and let's throw in a Gamma of 0.07. When the price of the underlying asset moves from $48 to $49, then the Delta of the option moves up to +0.52. Also, if the price falls from $48 to $47, then the Delta becomes 0.38.

So, both Delta and Gamma move in the same direction as they both essentially measure the same thing. Thus, one change in one means a similar effect in the other and thereby affects the price of the option itself.

Theta

The next Greek is Theta. Theta, as mentioned earlier, measure the phenomenon known as time decay. Theta is an estimate of how much the theoretical value of the option falls every day that there is no shift in the price of the underlying asset or volatility.

This is a measurement of how much an option's extrinsic value is chipped away given that all elements remain constant. Furthermore, Theta can measure the difference between calls and put. This depends on the cost that carrying the underlying asset may represent. For example, if such cost is positive (the dividend paid out is less than the interest rate) then the call is higher than the put. On the contrary, if the cost is negative (the dividend yield is greater than the interest rate), then call is less than the put. Also, long calls and puts have negative Theta while short calls and puts have positive Theta.

One thing to consider is that Theta has a greater effect on those options which has a shorter expiration date than those which have a longer expiration date.

For example, an option is due in 20 days. It has a value of $3.00 and a Theta of -0.15. Every day that passes without a change in volatility or the price of the underlying asset, then the price will drop by 15 cents on the dollar. So, the next day, the option would be worth $2.85.

Now, if the option has 80 days to maturity and a Theta of -0.03, all conditions remaining equal, the option's value would fall to $2.97 and so on.

Vega

The next Greek is Vega. This is also the only Greek that doesn't have an actual Greek letter attached to it (in case you were wondering).

Vega measures how much the theoretical value of an option would change for every 1% change in volatility. This Greek is rooted in the fact that higher volatility represents higher prices for the option. On the other hand, lower volatility means lower prices in the option. Hence, the reason why Theta is time decay. When there is higher volatility, the higher the probability that the option will make money on its expiration.

Long calls and puts have positive Vega, while short calls and puts have negative Vega. Zero Vega would mean that there have been no changes in the underlying stock price.

Now, let's consider the following:

An option has a value of $2.00. It has a Vega of +0.20 and volatility is measured at 30%. In this case, we assume that volatility rises to 31%. As such, the value of the option would rise to $2.20. On the other hand, if volatility falls to 29%, then the option would be valued at $1.80.

Consequently, there is a direct correlation between the price of the option and its volatility. As stated earlier, the price of an option is higher when there is greater volatility.

Rho

This Greek is the measure of how much the theoretical value of an option would move for every 1% in change to the interest rate. This implies that the Rho for a call and put option with the same strike price and maturity would not be the same.

Rho is not commonly used in those economies in which interest rates are stable. In those economies in which interest rates are variable, then Rho plays a much larger role.

In the case of the United States, interest rates move at a rather slow pace. Since they are not quite as volatile as in other parts of the world, it is worth mentioning that a change in interest rates would lead to the recalculation of Rho, and once all models are updated, the Rho would be left alone until the next change in rates.

For instance, an option has a price of $2.00 and a Rho of +0.02 with the underlying asset's price at $48 and interest rates at 5%. Now, suppose an increase to 6% on the interest rate. That would imply a rise in the price of the option to $2.02. Likewise, if interest rates dropped to 4%, then the price of the option would also drop to $1.98.

As you can see from this discussion on Greeks (without actually speaking Greek!), the calculation of each Greek variable allows investors to predict where prices are going to fall given the changes seen in each of the outlined conditions.

Your understanding of Greeks will allow you to figure out how you can make your moves in options and come out ahead. Also, the underlying theory that supports each Greek makes it easy to see how the moves in each of the variables that make up the Black-Scholes Model provides a fairly accurate picture of the pricing for each of the options you would like to analyze.

In addition, you can purchase the software that is used by the pros to run these numbers. However, your understanding of the math will enable you to actually understand what the numbers and therefore understand what you need to do.

Historical Volatility

As mentioned earlier, volatility is the fluctuation in prices of an underlying asset in the price of an options contract.

The basic tenet is that the higher the volatility, the higher the price of the option. Conversely, the lower the level of volatility, the lower the price of the option. As such, you tend to profit more when there are wild swings in the price of underlying assets as when there is little volatility.

Therefore, historical volatility becomes the measure of volatility itself over a given period of time. Please don't think that we are going to talk about volatility over months or even years. In fact, we are not even going to talk about weeks. In the majority of cases, we are going to be looking at volatility in terms of days. This is due to the fact that higher swings in prices lead to a faster tempo in trading over far shorter periods of time such as three or four days.

As have been discussed previously, options may be purchased for a matter of days or even hours. And while there are exotic options that contain perpetuity clauses, the fact remains that most options have a very short lifespan. So, when you get into the options market, you need to think in very short periods of time.

Historical volatility can be calculated over very short periods of time such as the 2-day average of the 10-day average. Most financial news channels and other financial data subscription services will provide you with the 2-day average. This is what is commonly displayed and it tracks the trend for the asset's price over that period. Price information may be updated hourly.

The measurement of historical volatility is what feeds the calculation of the Greeks. And of course, the Greeks feed the Black-Scholes Model of option price. Thus, having a close eye on volatility is an absolute must for those who are looking to invest in options.

How to Calculate Volatility

As described in the previous section, the calculation of historical volatility boils down to the measurement in the price of the underlying asset in question.

Assuming that the underlying asset is a stock, the changes in the price of that stock would fuel its volatility. Thus, if the stock's price does not fluctuate greatly or trades within a tight range, then volatility could be considered low. But if a stock begins trading above and below its 2-day average, then you would consider that there is volatility. By the same token, if the stock starts trading well above or below its 10-day average, then you would consider that to be high volatility.

Also, as you gain more experience as an investor, you will be able to recognize volatility just by looking at prices themselves at any given time. Over time, you will become familiar with the price of a stock, for example, and recognize the range that it trades in. When you see the stock's quote above, or below that range, then you will automatically know that volatility has picked up.

Furthermore, when you hear about certain news or hear reports of certain data, you may get the sense that volatility may pick up. This is when you can pounce.

For instance, the government's job report was lower than expected for the second quarter of the year. This economic data may have a negative impact on trading within a given sector. So, investors will be looking to get out of that sector and into one which had a positive impact from the jobs report.

Consequently, volatility will pick up on as investors try to get out from one sector and into another. What this means then is that you can cash in by taking out puts and calls. Hence, if you own stock in a sector which is rumored to get hammered, you can take out puts and set a strike price at a higher point. That way, you will protect your earnings on the sale of the actual stock.

Now, you could purchase a bunch of puts for that stock, without actually purchasing the stock itself, and then as volatility begins to pick up, you can dump those puts on the investors who are looking to get out. As the volatility picks up, the price of the puts goes up and you cash in.

Sure, the shift in prices may be pennies on the dollar as we saw in the previous examples, but when you multiply pennies on the dollar over thousands and thousands of puts, you can make a good chunk of change in a very short period of time.

Of course, this is a highly speculative situation as the impact of a negative job report by the government may not impact certain sectors as expected, thereby leaving you with no gain or even a loss due to the fact that volatility didn't pick up as expected.

Implied or Projected Volatility

Implied or projected volatility is an estimation of volatility based on the historical data available for a given asset.

As we have discussed, historical volatility is measured in short periods such as days. For the sake of implied volatility, you can take the 2-day average, though it would be best to use larger data sets such as the 10-day average or the 50-day average.

The reason for this is that the 2-day average may include peaks and valleys that are due to specific events which may, or may not, be fortuitous or even bizarre. Also, there are specific events, such as reports on economic data that directly impact the volatility of a given asset. Then, as the effect of the impact wear offs, volatility reverts back to its mean.

This is something very important which you must learn to recognize. Over longer periods of time, prices develop a pattern or trend. This is nothing more than its mean which can change over time. For example, an asset's price may have an increasing mean but then a sudden change can reverse the trend. This sudden event is something you would clearly see in the 2-day average, but then would fade away back into its mean.

However, over a 10-day period, or 50-day period, not to mention its 200-day average, you would clearly see the overall trend for that asset's price. As such, it's important for you to recognize these shifts in order to make wise decisions on where volatility is heading.

Consequently, implied volatility can be seen through the analysis of the trends in an asset's price.

You can clearly define a trend just by looking at the charts though the exact numbers would have to be calculated through validated formulas.

As I mentioned earlier, you can purchase the software that can calculate this figure, though most premium subscription services would offer you this data for the price of the subscription. So, I would encourage you to take a deeper look at how implied volatility can help you understand where prices of assets are heading, and thereby help you gain a more intuitive feel for where volatility may be headed. You can also learn to recognize which important events happen throughout the year or gain a sense of how singular events may affect markets such as Presidential elections.

As I have said throughout this book, it pays to do your homework.

Diminishing Risks in Options Trading by Using Greeks

One of the core tenets that I have mentioned throughout this book is that trading in the derivatives market implies a higher degree of risk. Consequently, you need to understand such risk and find ways to protect yourself against them.

This is why the biggest risk that you can find yourself with is volatility. Volatility can zap your gains in a heartbeat and even cause you to lose money. In the worst of cases, you can lose the shirt off your back if you make a gamble on a play that doesn't work.

So, what to do?

By using Greeks, you can get a better handle of where the risk of volatility will take. For instance, if you are expecting volatility to pick up in a given period of time, you can run your simulations to determine how the theoretical price of an option would look like given certain changes in the input variables of the model.

Consequently, you can determine what price points you are looking to get into, and which price points you are looking to get out of. This is the easiest and fastest way you can protect yourself against volatility.

However, you can take specific steps toward protecting yourself in a given situation.

When you have highly volatile asset prices, you can begin by taking out options which can rid of the highly volatile asset and then bring you back in when things have settled down.

Now, let's assume volatility in each of the Greeks. In a highly volatile Delta, that is changes in the price of the asset, then you can take out stop-loss orders in order to make sure that you don't get wiped out by volatile prices.

In the case of a highly volatile Gamma, you may want to look at taking out both long and short positions on the asset itself in order to make sure that you are covered either way.

As for Theta, if you see that asset prices look to be rather steady, then you might want to consider getting out of that option position altogether and purchase the asset itself, particularly if you are looking to get out of cash. Investors who live in countries where there is a considerable risk of cash becoming devalued will look to dump cash as much as possible and move into other assets which can hold their value. This is also true of highly inflationary environments.

Regarding Vega, when you detect higher levels of volatility, this is when you need to move fast and act. So, Vega, in itself, will not derail your strategy unless you are in the midst of a financial markets meltdown. In that case, you need to dump securities right away and move into physical assets such as commodities, land, metals, and equity of privately-owned companies.

In such environments, holding on to cash may help, but if a market crash is accompanied by inflation, then cash may not be very much use. However, if you are able to react quickly, you can pick up some bargains on the cheap. This is why holding highly liquid instruments can help you get out of them quickly, take your cash and then turn around and sink it into more tangible assets, which can hold wealth over the long run meanwhile the dust settles from the crash.

Finally, changes in Rho, that is interest rates, can wreak havoc on investors. When interest rates climb, you will see the price of your options rise and then when interest rates fall, the price of option is set to go down. Bear in mind that changes in Rho may be a good moment for you to take a position since investors may panic as to the outcome of those changes in interest rates and leave them looking to see where they can turn to. When you see that Rho is going up, you can take long positions. If you see that Rho is heading down, you can take short positions. This is a good way of looking at how you can hedge your position.

Mispricing Options

Pricing derivatives is a field for skilled mathematicians comparable to putting people on the moon. If you miss by an inch, you could be hurled into space forever.

The same goes with pricing options. If you are unable to get the pricing estimations right, then when you actually close the deals, you will not be getting the price you expected. This can lead you to losing the shirt of your back, or perhaps hitting a home run by accident. Of course, the chances of hitting a home run by accident are slim. So, it pays to get pricing down right.

This entire discussion on the pricing of options leads to one thing: building accurate projections based on the input factors which affect pricing to a point where you can accurately predict where prices are going to shift. This can then lead you to wise choices on the options you can purchase or sell.

Perhaps the worst fear for options traders is to purchase options that end up going down in price or selling options which still went up in price.

In both of those cases, you would lose money by either getting less out of the deal or leaving money on the table by selling too early. So, if you are serious about options trading, I would advise you to spend some money and get the software that you need in order to run these calculations. You can purchase data packs for Microsoft Excel which can run this data for you.

One word of caution: unless you are an expert in valuating derivatives, I would highly recommend you avoid running the numbers yourself. This is why there are the software packages available for this purpose.

Predicting big shifts in options price

Predicting, also known as forecasting, is perhaps the hardest thing to do in the business world. If there is anyone who could ever get this down to an exact science, they would not only win every Nobel Prize out there, but they would instantly become the richest person in the world.

When you build the models we have discussed in this chapter, what you are doing is building a model which can help you predict the changes in asset prices, and consequently, options prices. When you get this down cold, you can accurately predict where things are headed. Sure, you may be off by a few cents here and there, but you won't find yourself out in the cold. You will always be in the ballpark.

I should warn you that options are highly speculative endeavors which may cause you to expose yourself to risk. By understanding the ways in which we can measure risk, such as through the use of Greeks, you can set yourself up for success.

So, I hope that this chapter has given you the insight that you need in order to gain a clear understanding of how you can dabble in the options market and come out a winner every time.

Chapter 6: Getting Started with Options Trading

In this chapter, we are going to cover some of the basics regarding how you can get into options trading.

The core tenet of this type of trading lies in the role you want to play, that is, being a passive investor or being a more active investor.

If you are looking to remain passive, then perhaps options may not be the right choice for you. However, if you are looking to take on a more active role, then it would be good for you to explore this investment opportunity. After all, there are opportunities for you to get into this market every day.

How to Get Started

So, there are two general ways in which you can get started.

The first is for you to open an account with a traditional investment firm and have a professional money manager handle your trades. You can specify that you want exposure to options. There you can sit down with a money manager and go over your alternatives.

This would be a good choice for passive investors who want to get exposure to this type of investment strategy but may not be keen on actually getting their hands dirty. Not all investment firms may be so accommodating with their investors. So, you would have to shop around to see which investment firm would be willing to accommodate your requests.

The second, and by far the most effective, is to open a brokerage account.

When individual investors open brokerage accounts, they tend to fall under the "day trader" umbrella. For the sake of clarity, let's define what a day trader is.

A day trader is an individual investor who, through a brokerage account, buys and sells securities, among other investment instruments, but holds no open positions at the end of the trading day. That means that these investors open their positions when the trading day starts, go through their trading day, and then close everything for the night. This is especially true on Friday evenings. Day traders would rather jump out of a plane without a parachute then leave positions open over the weekend.

Being a day trader leads to making very short-term trades, often with a window of just a few hours. This is a great way of hedging against risk, though as we have discussed, things can change in a hurry. So, it pays to be on your toes all the time.

A good rule of thumb that I live by is that if you have open positions, then you need to be at your desk. If you decide that you want to take a long lunch break, then close everything and start back up during the afternoon session. By being away from your desk with open positions, you may end up getting clobbered without even realizing it.

For those investors who are willing to keep their positions open for longer than a day, the "swing trader" category befits them. These investors or traders would benefit from keeping positions open for longer than a day since they feel that the shifts in the markets would not happen overnight, but rather may take a couple of days.

Nevertheless, swing traders don't typically hold positions open for longer than a week. That means that they will open a position on Monday morning, for instance, and close on Friday evening. This would be the longest a typical swing trader would hold an open position.

That being said, you can choose to go either way depending on the circumstance you find yourself in. If you are new to the game, I would highly recommend that you start out with day trading and gradually build yourself up to more and more complex positions.

Options Trading Basics

So, once you have decided that you are going to become day or swing trader, you are ready to get started with your own account.

Brokerage accounts are offered by large investments banks and come in a wide range of colors and flavors. However, there are two main types of accounts.

- **A full-service account** - This account offers you access to the trading platform and all the analytics that come with it. All the bells and whistles in this type of account allow you to make the most informed decisions about your trades. However, they may have a high maintenance fee as all those analytics don't come free. Nevertheless, having access to all of those analytics will help you make informed decisions. Also, full-service accounts generally have a lower transaction cost. So, this is something to definitely keep in mind.

- **A discount brokerage account** - When you go the discount route, you are given access to the platform and all the trading that comes along with it, but without the bells and whistles. Therefore, you are basically on your own. You may only get access to the basic analytics, but not much beyond that. These accounts have lower maintenance fees but may also have higher transaction fees. So, you need to do your research as higher transaction fees may represent a higher cost to you especially when you make a large number of trades.

Ultimately, your choice of account lies in how comfortable you feel with your skill and knowledge about trading options.

It should be noted that you may not have access to trading options right away. You may have to build up a few successful trades before you are approved to start off with options. Or, you may have to wait a certain amount of time before you are ultimately cleared for options trading, among other derivatives such as ETFs and even futures.

Now, when you first open an account, you can get access to a practice account. This account is the real deal, but you are only doing "paper trading" that is, you are not actually playing with money.

What does that mean?

It means that if you win or lose, you won't actually be doing it with real money. Your gains and losses will be credited to an account which doesn't hold any real funds. This is a great way for you to learn the ropes of how the platform works.

Thus, doing paper trading means that you will have to invest time in learning how the platform works. In the end, though, you will be poised to start making money when you get down to the real thing.

As a matter of fact, I would encourage you to go down this road first. It will not only help you learn the ropes of how trading works, but it will also help build your confidence. This is very important since racking up losses in a simulation will not destroy your confidence as losing real money in the real thing. So, take the time to go through a practice account and learn the ropes of the trading platform you have chosen.

When you finally feel comfortable for the real thing, you can use limit order to help you keep your winnings in check.

Often, the transactions fees attached to a trade may be higher than what you actually make. So, you can use limit order to set your price for the options you are looking to purchase. When other investors hit these price points, then you can get yourself a deal. This will help you keep your profits in check.

As you gain more and more confidence, you will be able to make more successful deals. As your investable assets also grow, you will be able to make the most of your profits by reinvesting them into your account. At the end of the day, you will become more and more successful as you build momentum.

So I would encourage you to start off small and build your way up. That way, you can make the most of your investments by working through the learning curve before actually playing at the high-stakes table. Bear in mind that it is all a process. As such, you will need to take a few lumps before you really learn the ins and outs of the trading.

Buying and Selling Basics

At different points in this book you have seen me use the terms "open" and "closed" positions.

A position is when you engage in investing. If you have no investment, then you hold no position. It's not until you actually put your money to work that you actually have a position. In that regard, you have an open position when you purchase an investment. Consequently, your position is open while you hold that investment, and then it is closed when you sell it off and hold it no longer.

When you are actually trading positions, you generate a "market order". A market order is an order to buy or sell, that is, a call or put option. In general, most traders start off with "vanilla positions", that is, the standard put/call option. They don't come with any fancy add-ons and don't have any of the bells and whistles that exotic options have.

Now, with online trading, you can program your market orders so that they are triggered as soon as the strike price is hit, the maturity is reached, or you trade it manually. Whatever the condition, you can use the trading platform's automatic trading features to make your trades in real time. That way, you can track the trends in your options, but won't have to actually carry out the transaction manually. That can be done for you.

This is why I always say that you should never leave your open positions unattended.

Consider this situation:

You have placed several call options at a given strike price. When the asset hits that price, the market order is automatically generated and you have your asset. Now, let's say that you have decided to take a two-hour lunch and take a break from it all.

Fair enough, right?

Well, let's assume that your call option was one of the thousands of call options on that same asset. As such, the price spiked then other investors immediately turned around to dump their positions and cash in. Meanwhile, you were enjoying your lunch. By the time you get back, you find out what happened and realize that your asset is now under water.

You could have avoided that scenario by adding a stop-loss order to your asset so that it would trigger another put option once the asset hits the strike price you are looking to sell at. Now, depending on the platform, that may or may not be possible. For instance, you would have to take the position and then enter the stop-loss order in order to protect your position.

These are the minutiae which you need to look at when becoming familiar with your chosen platform. If you are unaware of how it all works, you could end up making a rookie mistake such as the one I have described.

So it pays to be careful with your open positions. When you exercise caution, you can take that two-hour lunch and enjoy life!

Making Sense of the Valuation of Options

In previous chapters, we had an extensive discussion on the valuation of options. Now, I don't expect you to be an expert on options valuation, at least not yet, but it certainly pays to do research and pay attention on how you can become proficient in the valuation of options.

As such, I would like to reiterate that the valuation of an option boils down to the volatility in the underlying asset. Please remember the axiom: the higher the volatility, the higher the option price. This is why volatility is now your new best friend. If you are able to make this work for you, then you will surely have a good chance to make some decent returns in the options game.

However, if you are not able to fully grasp the way options work, then I would suggest that you either seek professional financial advice or perhaps find another type of investment which you feel more comfortable with.

The legendary investor Warren Buffet once said that you need to deal with businesses you understand.

Personally, I believe this to be quite true. You cannot be truly successful at a business you don't fully understand. This is why it is important for you to make the time and effort to drill down and get to the core of your financial trading strategy. That way, when you engage in options trading, you will be able to make the most of it.

Also, when dealing with pricing, spending a few bucks on good valuation software can help you visualize where you want to go with your options strategy. Often this means having to run simulations in your computer so that you can forecast where you are going to set your positions.

That being said, it is also important for you to understand the underlying aspects to options valuation and the input factors that generate the ultimate price such as the Greeks.

I would also encourage you to make friends with like-minded individuals who have more experience than you do in the options game. They can give you pointers in the right direction and help you avoid some common pitfalls and potential dangers.

For me, it was very educational to learn from others who were more experienced than me. They helped me to see the forest for the trees. This meant that I was able to learn from their experience and also from their mistakes.

I hope that by reading this book, you are able to learn from my experience. It has taken me years to gain mastery of this topic, so now I hope that you too can learn from me.

Strategies for Buying/Selling Options

The basic strategy when it comes to trading options is to buy low and sell high. This axiom is as old as time itself.

Now, actually buying low and selling high depends on what you are doing to find those options which you can turn around and sell at a profit.

This is why the first step in the options game is for you to find good assets which you can buy low, place your options into place, and then sell when the time has come.

Of course, there are other types of options out there which you can engage in. Let's have a look at a couple of these.

Naked and covered options

A naked option is when you purchase an option for a stock or asset which you do not own. As such, you can make money when you buy low and sell high on the asset. So, if you place the option, the price falls, you purchase, and then you turn around and sell the asset before you are required to cover your position, you can make money without needing to shell out a dime.

Now, this type of transaction is risky and represents potential for disaster when the investor is required to cover the position and does not have the funds to do so. This may lead to a brokerage account being suspended.

A covered position is when you have the funds to cover a position or to purchase the asset in question.

Let's look at an example:

An investor chooses to place a call option for a stock in XYZ corporation. The investor sets a strike price of $5 per share. When the strike price is hit, then the purchase order is placed. Now, the investor does not actually have the funds to cover the position. There is a lag between the time the order is placed and the time the funds need to be delivered.

From the time the option is placed to the time the funds need to be delivered, the investor can place a put option to sell when the price reaches $5.50. When the time comes to cover their position, the investor has the proceeds from the sale to cover his earlier position.

This scheme has the potential for disaster if the time comes and the investor does not have the funds to cover their position. The put option did not go through as expected. Now, the investor needs to come up with the funds needed in order to cover such position.

Needless to say, this type of transaction is risky. That is why I always recommend investor to have some cash put away in order to cover any open positions which may lead to potential insolvency. Naturally, a consistent pattern of this type of behavior will cause investors to lose their good standing within the market and may cause their account to be suspended. In that case, the brokerage firm may require the investor to put funds down as a guarantee of good faith that they will be able to cover future positions.

Exercising options

Options can be exercised through order.

There are four main types of orders.

- **Market order**. This type of order is the main type of order. This can be a buy or sell order. All orders are market orders since they are placed in order to carry out a transaction. When the transaction goes through, the order is exercised. Market orders can be placed ahead of time, hence the option and may be canceled if the investor changes their mind based on prevailing market conditions.

- **Limit order**. This is the type of order in which the investor agrees on the price, but not the execution. As such, the order may or may not be executed. This type of order is good for novice investors in the options market. These orders are the best way to limit exposure to price volatility, both to underlying assets as well as options themselves.

- **Stop-loss order**. This type of order is placed when the investor wants to set a limit to the potential losses the investor may face due to a decline in the market conditions. So, the investor sets a strike price in which they are comfortable. The order will become converted into a put option when the strike price is triggered, the market order is then issued, and the deal goes through.

- **Stop-limit order**. This is similar to a stop-loss order. The difference is that the stop-limit order pulls the plug on the limit order when a given strike price is triggered. If such price is triggered, then the deal may still go through rather than being axed.

Advanced Options Trading Strategies

In this section, we are going to be looking at the Butterfly spread. This is an advanced options strategy that can help you make some interesting deals.

So, let's have a closer look.

The butterfly spread consists of purchasing options in 1-2-1 ratio. For instance, if the investor purchases one call option at a given strike price, and then sell two calls at a higher price. Since the investor now has an unbalanced position, the investor must now purchase a second call at the lower price in order to cover the call that was sold.

This strategy is complex since the investor is speculating with selling call options in order to avoid leaving a naked position. As such, the investor can hold one position in order to set the market order in place. When the naked position is taken on, then the investor needs to cover the back end of their position.

This implies that the investor is speculating that the second position they are covering will fall in price. Otherwise, they may lose money on the deal.

Another example of this strategy is called shorting.

In shorting a position, the investor sells calls or puts, but does not actually own any positions. When the sale goes through, the investor needs to deliver the position. At this time, the investor needs to make sure they have the means to cover that position. If the sale price ends up being lower than the purchase price, the investor will have lost on the deal.

In essence, what shorting plays off is that the massive selloff in positions will trigger a decline in the price. At that point, the investor can purchase the positions needed in order to cover the sale. Needless to say, this is highly speculative and can lead to serious complications for investors who do not have the funds or the positions to cover their shorts.

Final thoughts

Since these types of transactions tend to be highly speculative, investors should take care to ensure that they have the means to cover their positions. A worst-case scenario might be having to sell off other assets in order to cover naked positions. Therefore, uncovered positions are highly risky for investors. Thus, it is vital that you have all contingencies in place so that when the time comes to cover your positions, you are ready to do so.

Finally, it is also worth mentioning that as you become proficient in this type of trading, you can make very good gains when the market conditions are right. Of course, this requires you to keep your eyes and ears open at all time since opportunities may be right around the corner.

Chapter 7: Tips and Strategies for Options Trading

In this final chapter, we will be looking at some good tips and strategies to put into practice as part of your daily trading routine.

When engaging in options trading, the best way for you to achieve your peace of mind is to tie up all of your loose ends and ensure that you have contingencies in place, to make sure that you have everything you need to cover your positions in case anything should happen.

So, let's have a look at some tips and strategies.

Best Practices in Options Trading

The following are pieces of advice which I would like to share with you so that you can have some pointers to keep in mind in addition to all the various points we have described throughout this book.

1. When you engage in options trading, you don't necessarily need to have cash on hand in order to make deals happen. However, you will need to have enough cash in reserves in case you need to cover a position which didn't go through in time such as the case of naked options. Leaving naked or uncovered options may cause an investor to find themselves in a

tough spot and lose money on a deal that didn't work out as expected.

2. Become familiar with technical analysis. By becoming familiar with technical analysis, you will be able to engage in trading with a very good sense of where you are going and what you are doing. In addition, you will have a good sense of what to expect and what not to engage in. As such, it pays to spend a few dollars on a good analytics package or subscription which can help you stay on top of the latest information available to you.

3. Don't be afraid to get into software used for value options. Since the valuation of options can get really tricky, especially when taking all of the Greeks into account, it will be very hard for you to build your own spreadsheets and run the numbers yourself. In fact, it may take you a long time before you can actually get the handle on the proper valuation of options. Luckily, there are specialized software packages or suites for Microsoft Office which you can use to calculate and forecast the price of options. This can help you produce an accurate picture of what to

expect when you engage in these types of transactions. Furthermore, your understanding of valuation can help you get a good handle on where prices lie and if they are a good value.

4. Set limit orders especially when you are first starting out. Since limit orders agree on the price but don't hold an obligation to go through on the deal, you can be sure that you can make the deal that's right for you. In doing this, you can protect yourself from going through on a deal that may not be right for you. It also gives you the option of backing out on a deal in which circumstances have changed and may no longer be right for you.

5. Use stop-loss orders whenever possible. Stop-loss orders are a great way for you to set a strike price with which you can limit any potential losses you may face. This makes a great way of protecting your deals so that you do not, inadvertently, miss the opportunity to sell while you still make a profit or reach your breakeven point. Stop-loss orders are one of the best ways in which you can protect yourself.

Common Pitfalls to Avoid

1. Please bear in mind that when you have open positions, you need to be on top of them at all times. Often, investors feel confident when they set up all of their electronic reminders and settings in order to automate puts and calls based on strike prices and so on. Since markets are so dynamic, falling asleep at the wheel may cause you to miss out on some good opportunities especially in periods of high volatility. So, it pays to keep your eyes on the ball at all times. If you are looking to take a break, then you can close your positions and call it day.

2. Also, it's important to track your positions once you have taken them on. Options trading is not the kind of trading in which you can set an automatic timer and forget about it. If you have an open position, track it, since you may not be sure of what can happen. You can always kill orders before they are triggered. So, having a good business intelligence subscription will help you stay on top of your orders and help you make the right decisions when the time comes.

3. Another pitfall is engaging in a trade when you don't have all the information you need or when valuations look fishy. In such cases, it's better to steer clear as you may end up making a mistake by basing your decision on flawed analytics. This is especially true when you don't get the price right. In that case, if your instincts or logic tells you that the valuation of an option is off, then don't get into the deal. You may end up regretting it later.

4. It is also vital that you spend the time learning how valuations are done, but it is also important that you do not make it a regular habit of valuating every deal you make yourself. Of course, having an understanding of the underlying math and theory is essential. However, valuating deals yourself is not only time consuming but may lead to potential flaws due to human error. By using computer software designed to that extent, you can ensure that you are using the right methodology. This will enable you to double check on any valuations you see out there in the market.

5. The last pitfall I would like to point out is disregarding the Greeks. When you begin your options trading career, it's easy to overlook the Greeks. I know that it's one of the geekier parts of trading, but it shouldn't have to be. You can learn about the Greeks in a rather easy and digestible manner. I cannot stress enough the importance of making sure that you have a keen understanding of these variables so that you can truly maximize your full understanding of these indicators.

By taking these pitfalls into consideration, you will not only be able to sidestep them, but also be able to make the most of your investment opportunities. At the end of the day, you will learn as much from your own mistakes as you will from others. Of course, it is always best to learn from the mistakes of others so you can avoid making them yourself.

Getting a Handle on the Psychology of Options Trading

The final point I would like to make in this book is to beware of the psychology behind options trading.

There is a powerful psychological component that goes into trading securities, commodities, bonds, and especially derivatives.

When you engage in this type of trading, it's often easy to follow the crowd. You may even end up getting hot tips on stocks and business deals which promise amazing returns. Sure, they are out there, but by the time everyone is in on them, the ship has already sailed. When you see that all sorts of investors are flocking to a deal, it is because you are most likely getting in at the top.

What does that mean?

That there is no place to go but down.

So, always take any advice and tips you get with a grain of salt. If your judgment and intuition tell you that it's a good deal, then you can be confident that, at least of the surface, it looks good. But you should always do your homework. You have the information and the technical tools to help you follow up on these ideas and make sure that you have the right idea in place.

Also, psychology can lead people to do crazy things. The world is filled with investors who are looking to hit it out of the park. And yes, there are a few who have. But hitting a home run every time is not possible. So, you must make sure that you put a good swing on the ball when the pitch is right, and also take care of not striking out because you swung at the wrong pitch.

I know the baseball analogy may seem a bit drastic, but it is your understanding of the markets that will help you keep your cool and avoid making crazy mistakes because you got caught up in the buzz surrounding a deal.

At the end of the day, your intuition, experience, judgment, and common sense will help keep you grounded in the right opportunities which you can exploit to your benefit and that of your loved ones. After all, your gains and successes will also be those of your loved ones.

Conclusion

Well, we have made it to the end of this journey.

Indeed, options trading is an extensive topic that deserves a great deal of attention and study. You cannot expect to master this type of investment activity in a short period of time. But that doesn't mean it should take you forever either.

So, I would encourage you to do as much research as you can on this topic. In doing so, you will be building your business acumen. Since we are not born knowing everything, your understanding of these potentially complex transactions will help you gain keen insights, and thereby, an edge over other investors.

While it is true that this isn't a competition, it is a race toward your own goals. So, the faster you can get there, the better you will feel about yourself, your life, and the more you can provide for your loved ones.

Now, whether you are a brand-new investor or a seasoned veteran, I would encourage you to go back and review any of the parts in this book that you feel you need to drill down deeper on. As always, I would love to hear from you and learn more about what you have to say about the topics covered in this book. I am more than happy to provide you with some additional pointers that we didn't cover in this book.

Please bear in mind that experience is the best teacher. So, your experience in this line of business will help you gain a clear insight as to what works and what doesn't. When you reach that point, you will become so comfortable with these trades, that it will seem like you are literally making money in your sleep.

Naturally, the learning curve in trading takes time. However, this book is an attempt at flattening that curve. Therefore, you won't have to spend years going through trades, making mistakes, and learning from them. The knowledge that has been distilled in this book is precisely the result of all those mistakes made by others before us. So, I would encourage you to learn from them and build on them.

As we approach the end of this book, I have nothing more to say than thank you.

Thank you very much for getting all the way to the end of this book. I know that there are a million other things you could have been doing, and other options out there which you could have read. Yet, you read my book and that is the best validation that an author can get. I am deeply humbled by you taking the time to read my words.

As always, I would encourage you to leave a review so that others who are interested in this book will have an honest opinion about what this book is all about. Your honest opinions and comments will be very helpful to all those who are looking to engage in options trading.

So, thank you once again and happy trading!

Finally, if you found this book useful in any way, a review on Amazon is always appreciated!